PIANO/VOCAL SELECTIONS

The Shubert Organization   Elizabeth Ireland McCann LLC
Bill Kenwright   Chase Mishkin   Terry Allen Kramer   Barbara & Buddy
Broadway Across America   Emily Fisher Landau   Peter May   Boyet
Larry Hirschhorn   Janet Pailet/Steven Klein   Elie Hirschfeld/Jed Be
Spring Sirkin/Ruth Hendel   Vasi Laurence/Pat Flicker Addiss   Wendy Federman/
Joey Parnes Executive Producer

In Association with
The Public Theater
and
The Berkeley Repertory Theatre

Presents

PASSING STRANGE

Book & Lyrics By   Music By
STEW   **STEW AND HEIDI RODEWALD**

Starring

STEW

with

**DE'ADRE   EISA   COLMAN   CHAD   REBECCA
AZIZA   DAVIS   DOMINGO   GOODRIDGE   NAOMI JONES**

and

DANIEL BREAKER

Scenic Design   Costume Design   Lighting Design   Sound Design
DAVID   **ELIZABETH**   **KEVIN**   **TOM**
KORINS   **HOPE CLANCY**   **ADAMS**   **MORSE**

Music Supervision & Orchestrations   Music Coordinator
STEW & HEIDI   **SEYMOUR**
RODEWALD   **RED PRESS**

Casting   Production Stage Manager
JORDAN and **HEIDI**   **TRIPP**
THALER   GRIFFITHS   **PHILLIPS**

Press Representative   Company Manager   Associate Producer
SAM RUDY   **KIM**   **S.D.**
MEDIA RELATIONS   **SELLON**   **WAGNER**

Choreography By
KAROLE ARMITAGE

Directed by and Created in Collaboration with
ANNIE DORSEN

Originally Presented by Berkeley Repertory Theatre: Tony Taccone Artistic Director, Susan Medak Managing Director
and The Public Theater: Oskar Eustis Artistic Director, Mara Manus Executive Director.

ISBN 978-1-4234-6282-8

HAL•LEONARD®
CORPORATION

7777 W. Bluemound Rd. P.O. Box 13819 Milwaukee, WI 53213

In Australia Contact:
Hal Leonard Australia Pty. Ltd.
4 Lentara Court
Cheltenham, Victoria, 3192 Australia
Email: ausadmin@halleonard.com.au

Visit Hal Leonard Online at
www.halleonard.com

"It is not only one of the best cast albums in memory, it is the CD-download of the year."

– EDGE Magazine

"The original cast recording...preserves the songs' acerbic sting and dynamic whirl of New Wave snarl ("Sole Brother"), skewered vaudeville ("The Black One") and shape-shifting soul ("Keys")."

– Rolling Stone

Passing Strange Original Broadway Cast Recording.
Available on Ghostlight Records.

www.ghostlightrecords.com

PROLOGUE
(We Might Play All Night)

Lyrics by STEW
Music by STEW and HEIDI RODEWALD

Moderate Blues Rock

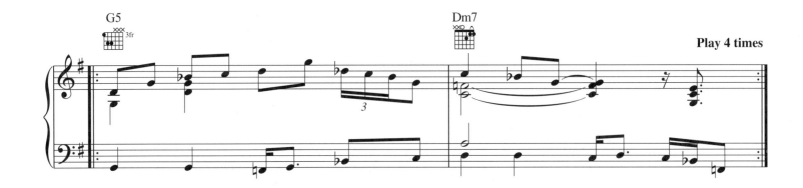

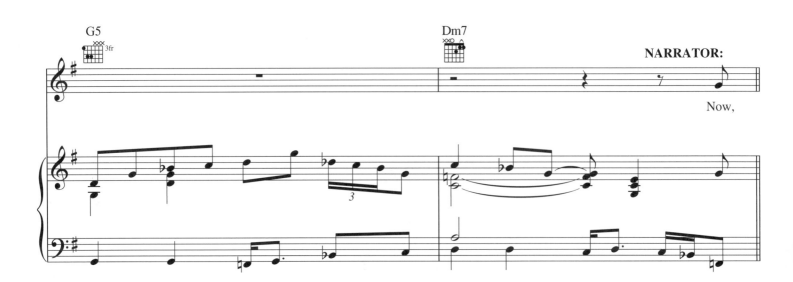

ARLINGTON HILL

Lyrics by STEW
Music by STEW and HEIDI RODEWALD

MUST HAVE BEEN HIGH

Lyrics by STEW
Music by STEW and HEIDI RODEWALD

MOM SONG

Lyrics by STEW
Music by STEW and HEIDI RODEWALD

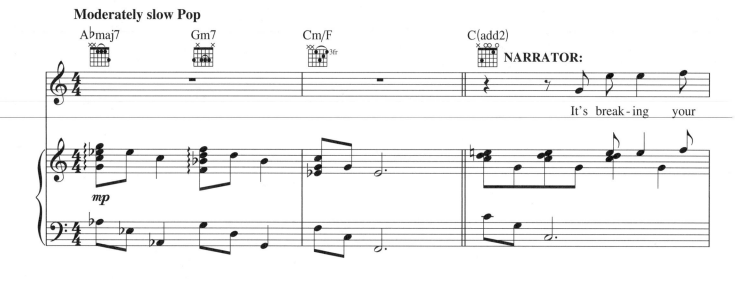

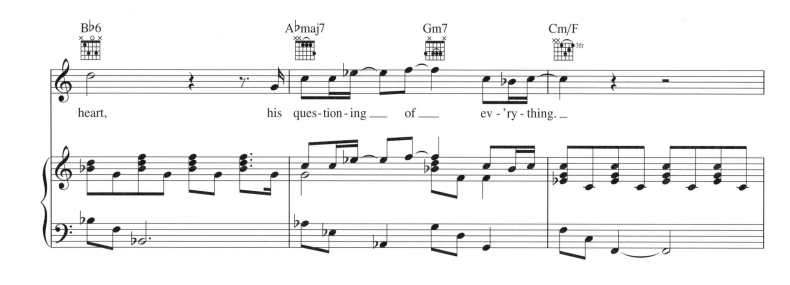

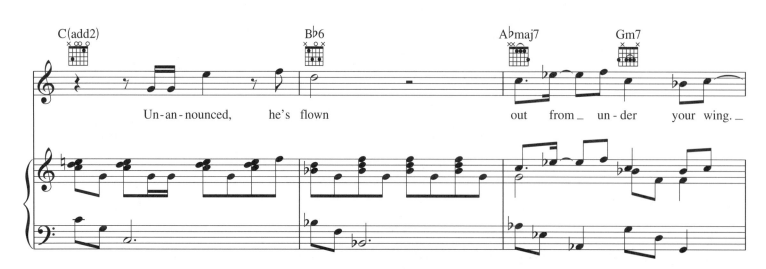

MERCI BEAUCOUP, M. GODARD

Lyrics by STEW
Music by STEW and HEIDI RODEWALD

AMSTERDAM

Lyrics by STEW
Music by STEW and HEIDI RODEWALD

KEYS

Lyrics by STEW
Music by STEW and HEIDI RODEWALD

hope you find _ it com-fort-a-ble, _ so please, take my keys. The

fau-cets leak, _ the cup-board's bare, _ my un-der-wear are ev-'ry-where, but

please, take my keys, take my keys.

YOUTH:

And af-ter

so long __ feel-ing so a-lone, __ I feel like pick-ing up the phone _ and

44

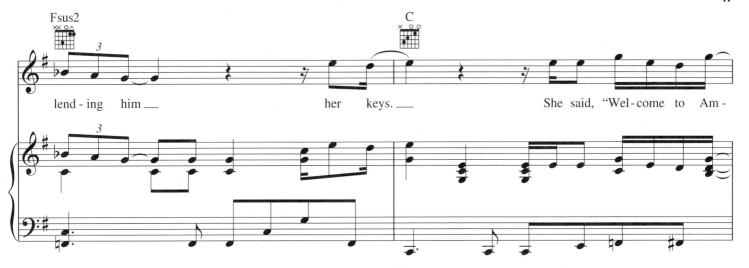

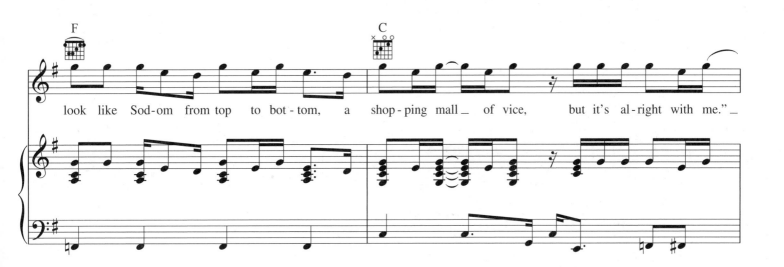

WE JUST HAD SEX

Lyrics by STEW
Music by STEW and HEIDI RODEWALD

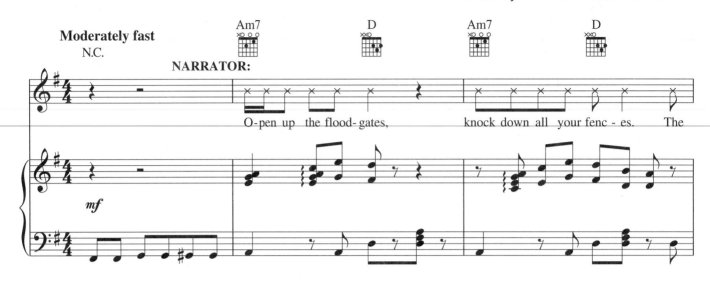

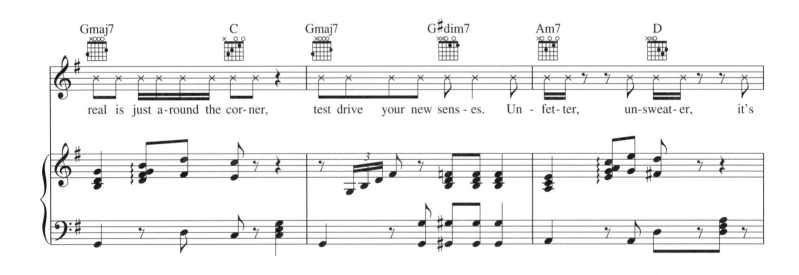

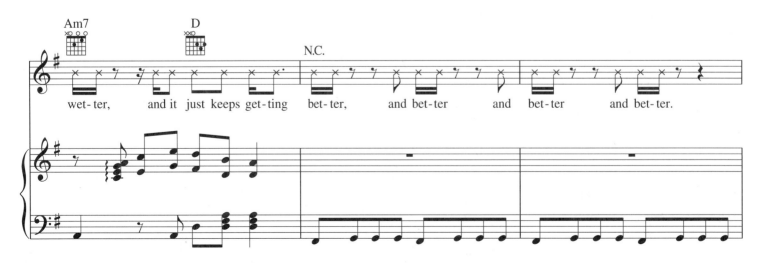

*Men sing where written

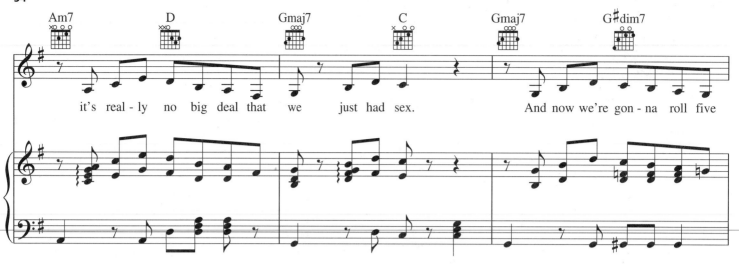

it's real-ly no big deal that we just had sex. And now we're gon-na roll five

big cig-a-rettes and have a cup of cof-fee.

YOUTH:

I

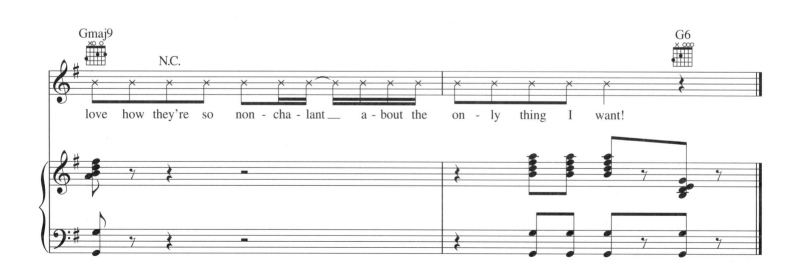

love how they're so non-cha-lant___ a-bout the on-ly thing I want!

STONED

Lyrics by STEW
Music by STEW and HEIDI RODEWALD

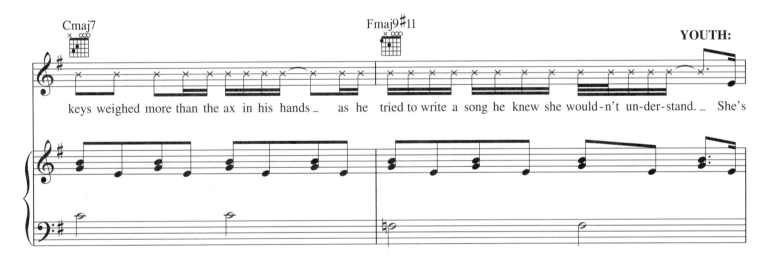

MOTHER:

dise is a bore. ___ It does-n't e-ven mat-ter an-y - more. ___

You gon-na ask me how I'm do - ing, or don't you care? ___ I'm

bored out of my mind ___ and what do you do ___ o-ver there? ___

Hav-ing a big ___ old house ___ should make a wom-an sing, ___ "La la la la la la la la." But

YOUTH:

Ma-ma, _____ Ma-ri - an-na and Mo-roc-can hash _ have got _ me stoned _

and I can't _ find my _ way home. _

MOTHER:

Wel-come to Am - ster-dam. _____ Wel-come to Am - ster-dam. _

Ma-ma, _____ she's serv-ing ev-'ry one of my de - sires _ on a plat-ter, but it does-n't e-ven mat-ter an-y-

more. _____ Oh, _____ par - a - dise is a bore. _____ It does-n't e - ven mat-ter an - y-

more. _ Oh, _____ par - a - dise is a bore. _____ It does-n't e - ven mat-ter an - y-

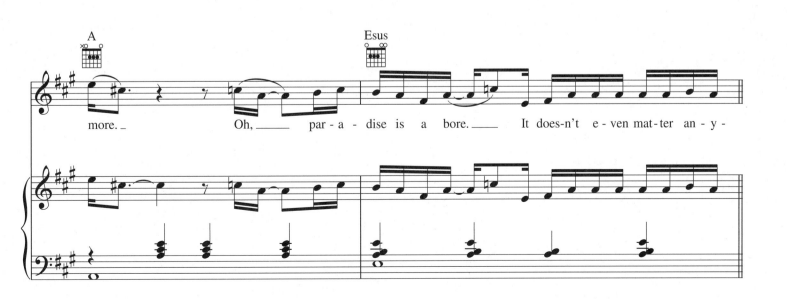

more. _ Oh, _____ par - a - dise is a bore. _____ It does-n't e - ven mat-ter an - y-

THE BLACK ONE

Lyrics by STEW
Music by STEW and HEIDI RODEWALD

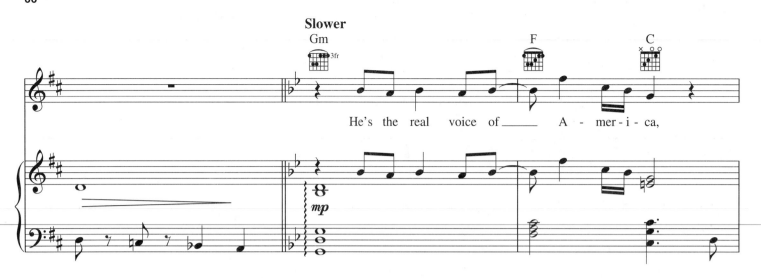

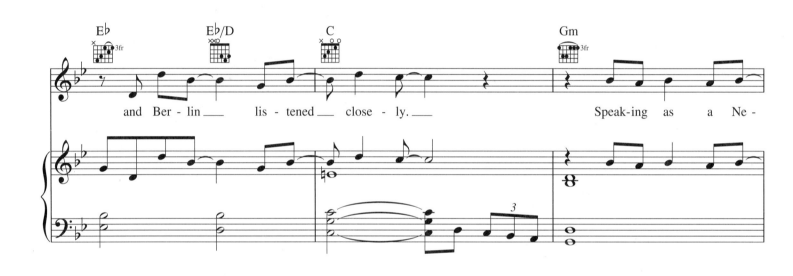

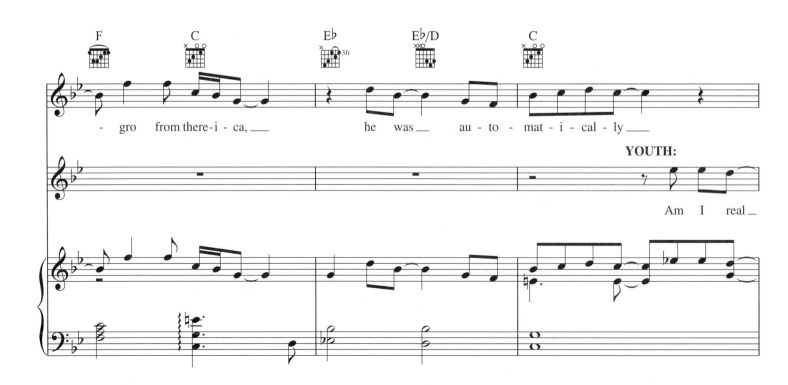

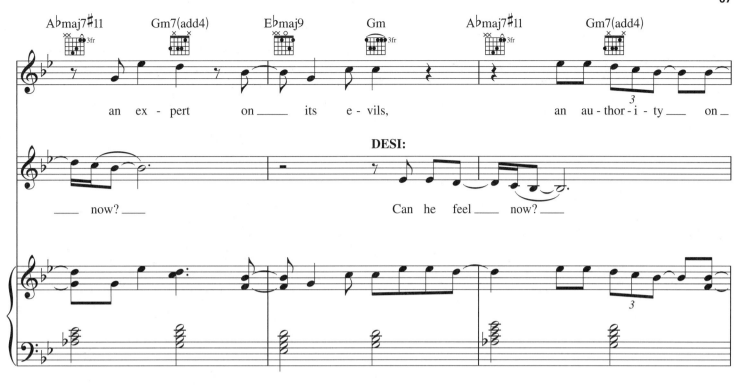

knowl-edge was al-most em-pir-i-cal___ of op-pres-sion from the pres-ent back to

slav-er-y times.___ Yah kah kah kah kah kah kah kah

kah kah kah kah!___ Who lets us know that we're in the right place?___ The

COME DOWN NOW

Lyrics by STEW
Music by STEW and HEIDI RODEWALD

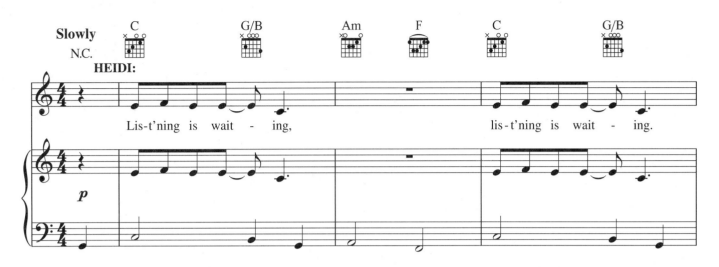

Slowly

HEIDI: Lis-t'ning is wait - ing, lis-t'ning is wait - ing.

Now you are __ knee deep __ in your __ head's foot - notes and your eyes __ are clos - ing.

I'll take your com-plex __ out of __ con - text __ and you can stop __ your pos - ing.

A little faster

DESI:

I've been lis - t'ning to ___ you talk - ing in ___ your sleep, it's a strange po - et - ry. You're

al - ways run - ning from ___ some - thing ___ it seems. ___

Let me chase a - way ___ what - ev - er's hurt - ing you, just have to ask it of ___ me.

My love is ___ more real ___ than all ___ your dreams. ___   'Cause

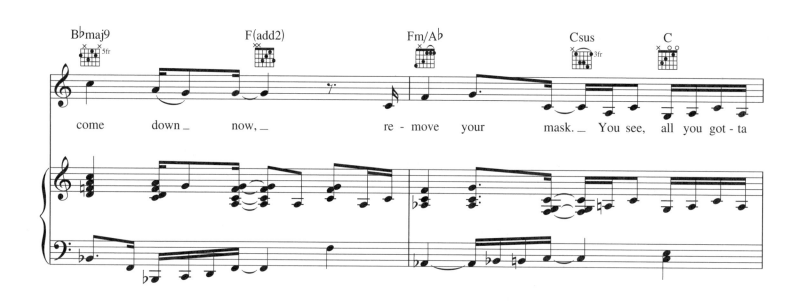

do is ask __ me, __ all you got - ta... Right when it was start-ing to feel __ real.

Love raged like an o - cean in a state of with-draw'l.

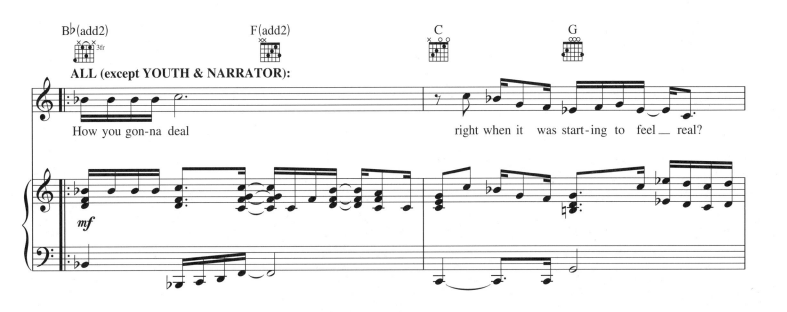

ALL (except YOUTH & NARRATOR):

How you gon-na deal right when it was start-ing to feel __ real?

How you gon-na deal right when it was start-ing to feel __ real? Why you wan-na leave?

YOUTH'S UNFINISHED SONG

Lyrics by STEW
Music by STEW and HEIDI RODEWALD

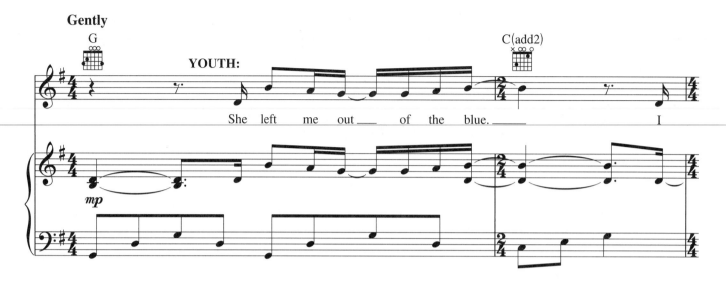

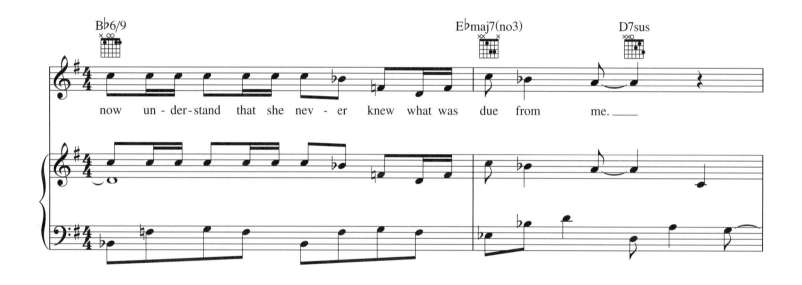

WORK THE WOUND

Lyrics by STEW
Music by STEW and HEIDI RODEWALD

lift my voice till I lift the curse, _ it's all re-hearsed, you see. _

This mu-sic al - ways res - cues me. _

There's a mel-o-dy for _ ev-'ry mal-a-dy, _ pre-scrip-tion

song, you _ see. _ And should the mask _ be-gin _ to fall, _

CUE MUSIC

Lyrics by STEW
Music by STEW and HEIDI RODEWALD

LOVE LIKE THAT

Lyrics by STEW
Music by STEW and HEIDI RODEWALD

Gentle Rock Ballad

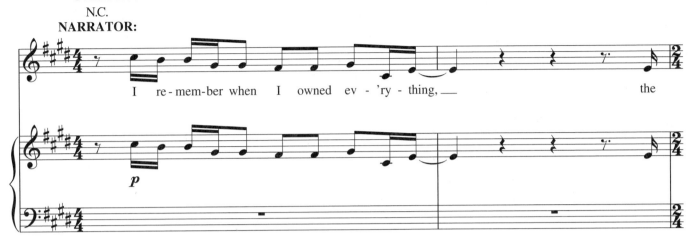

I re-mem-ber when I owned ev-'ry-thing, _____ the

sun and the moon and the rain, and my do-main _____

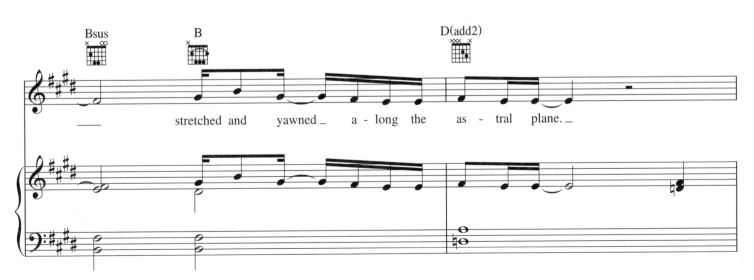

_____ stretched and yawned _ a-long the as-tral plane. _____